FLOWERS
Colouring Book

© Durlabh eSahitya Corner

Durlabh eSahitya Corner

1

Orange Canna Flower Colouring Page

Aster Flower Colouring Pages

Pink Camellia Flower Colouring Page

Turkish Flower Colouring Page

Purple Carnation Flower Colouring Page

Ornamental Babys Breath Flower Colouring Page

Chrysanthemum Colouring Page

Begonia Plant Colouring Page

Velvet Cockscomb Colouring Page

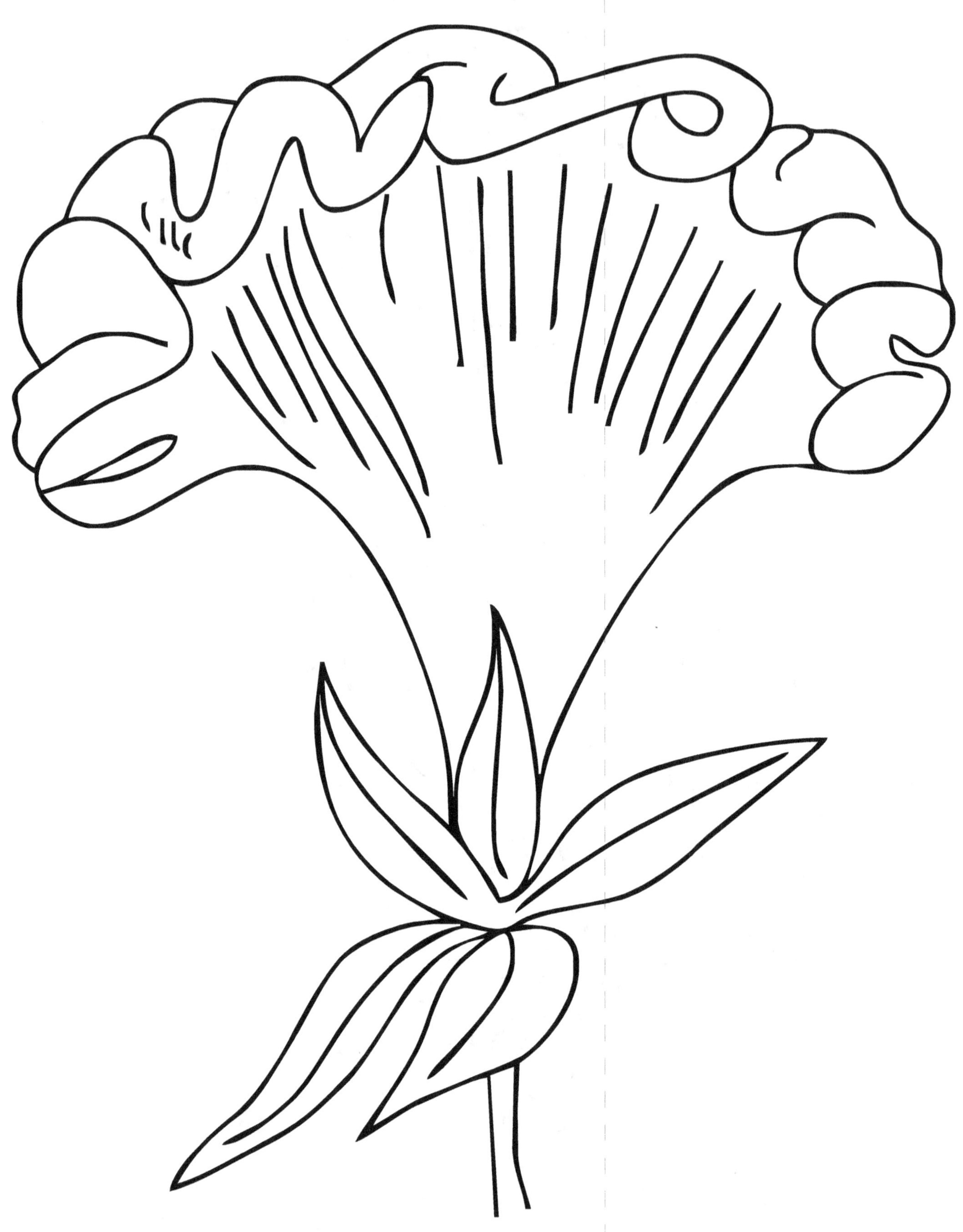

Bell Flower Colouring Page

Wild Columbine Flower Colouring Page

Bindweed Flowers Colouring Page

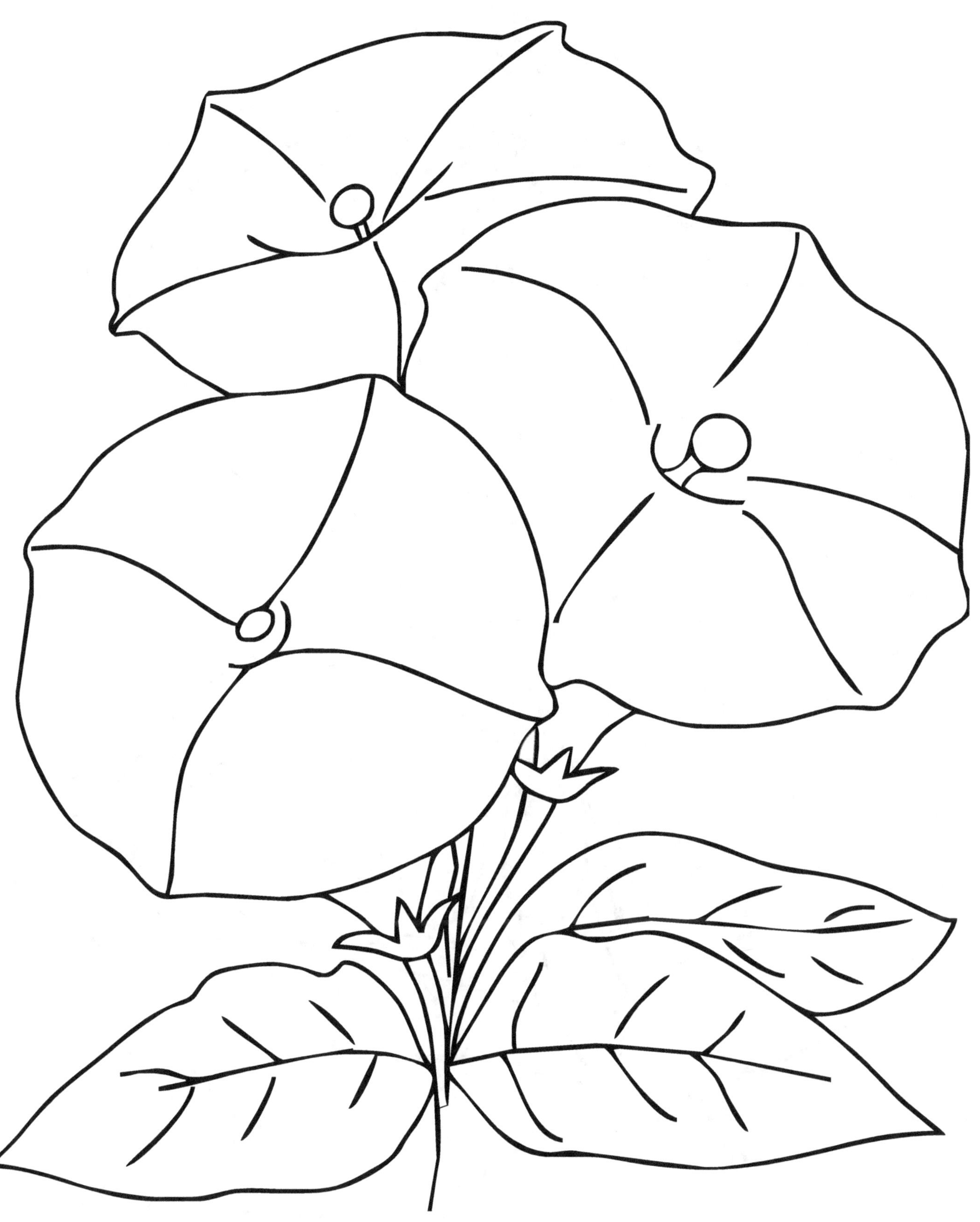

Cone Flower Colouring Page

Bindweed Morning Glory Colouring Page

Bunch of Cornflower Colouring Page

Growing Black Eyed Susan
Colouring Page

Purple Cosmos Flower Colouring Page

A Buttercup Flower Coloring Page

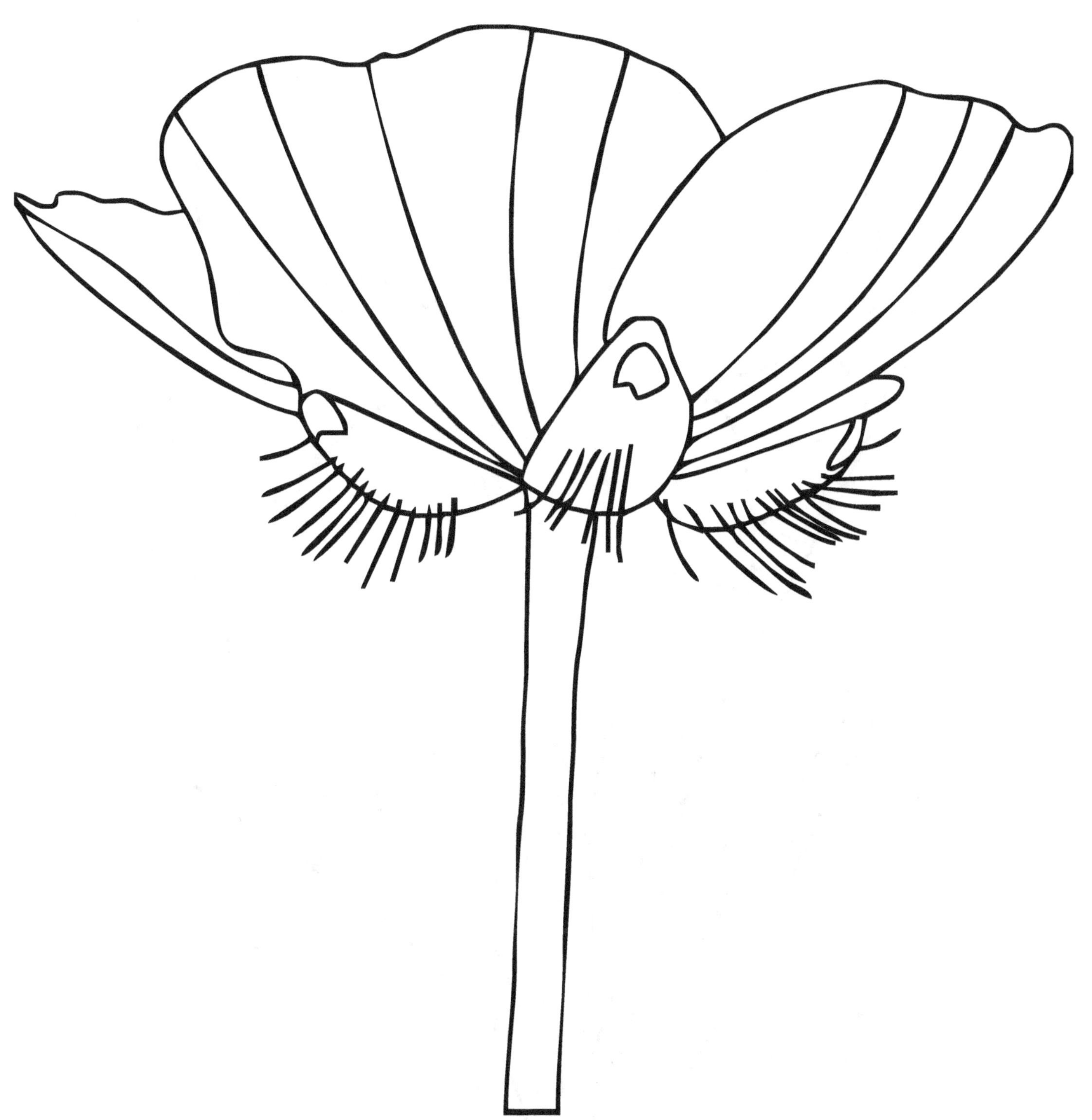

Yellow Daffodil Flower Colouring Page

Cactus Flower Colouring Page

Garden Flower Dahlia Colouring Page

Camellia Flower Colouring Page

Small Cactus Plant Colouring Page